THE FORT BEAUFORT U.F.O.

Guy Maasdorp.

ISBN 978-1-4478-4198-2.

THE FORT BEAUFORT U.F.O.

A TRUE STORY

REFERENCES:

U.F.O'S- Where do they come from? Editor: Peter Brookesmith.

The U.F.O. Phenomenon. Time Life Books, Amsterdam.

Mysteries of the unexplained Readers Digest.

Mysteries of the world- Editor Christopher Puik, Forward by Ian Wilson.

Readers Digest Illustrated Guide To South Africa.

The Internet.

INTRODUCTION:

On the banks of the Kat River is Fort Beaufort, the centre of a citrus farming area. The town originated in 1823 as a military stronghold and was named after the Duke of Beaufort, the father of Lord Charles Somerset, governor of the Cape. The fort still stands. On 7 January 1851 it withstood a full-scale assault by Xhosa warriors.

The mess house of the officers of the garrison is used as a museum, packed with guns, military uniforms and badges. An odd relic from the officer's mess is a square-shaped piano.

From Fort Beaufort the military road, known as the Queen's Road crosses the Great Fish River Valley to Grahamstown. This was completed in 1842 and provided the British with quick access to the troubled frontier.

Fort Beaufort is approximately 70km from Grahamstown and it's co-ordinates are 30 degrees latitude and 30 degrees longitude. This single fact becomes extremely important as this remarkable, true story unfolds.

This small town has many ghostly stories, strange happenings and unusual lights in the night sky.

Bob Burnell and his wife were driving back to Fort Beaufort after visiting friends in Grahamstown when this strange incident occurred. "It was a perfect, clear, calm day with no other cars on the road- we were about 15km outside Fort Beaufort when we both spotted a British Soldier sitting on the side of the road in his full 18th century regalia." "The man got up, ran across the road and simply disappeared into thin air." They both turned towards each other and exclaimed at the same time- "Did you see that?"

This and many other strange tales personifies the town of Fort Beaufort.

[Bob Burnell is the second degree witness to the Fort Beaufort U.F.O]

FORWARD:

In 1971 South Africa test exploded her first nuclear weapon- Those vibrations were felt around the world and throughout the universe. The vibrations are very similar to the vibrations felt when an earthquake strikes and are picked up by the same instruments. The aliens had to step in to put earthlings back on the right path .

This was the dawn of the computer era.

The "truth" came one July morning. Most sleepy South Africans did not see it or chose to ignore it, believing instead the so-called truth's contained in their religious text's.

No human being walks this earth without seeking the "truth". They will peruse and study their particular religious texts but never once look skyward.

WITNESS TESTIMONY:

First Degree Witness- directly involved in witnessing anything to do with the events surrounding the Fort Beaufort U.F.O.

Second Degree Witness- relating the story from someone who was directly involved.

[Most names have been changed to protect the people involved.]

Some First Degree Witnesses have passed away at the time of writing this book.

The farmer on whose farm the U.F.O. landed passed away in Port Alfred in December, 2009.

The Captain in the South African Airforce who shot down the U.F.O. is retired and lives with his wife in Pretoria in magnificent opulence.

South Africa remains the only country in the world to have shot down a U.F.O. The essence of this remarkable story was

related to me by Second Degree Witnesses.

OBSTACLES AND DIFFICULTIES

Due to the time period elapsed (40 years), I was unable to obtain newspaper reports of this event from the archives of Times Media L.t.d.

Although Radio Algoa had an interview with two key witnesses in November, 2008, they informed me that they do not keep records of these interviews. Fortunately I committed most of that interview to memory. Interestingly enough that particular interview was cut short. (By the government?)

[All over the world governments have threatened to take away a radio station's broadcasting license for reporting U.F.O. activity.] Why?

AUTHOR INDEMNITY:

Views, Theories and Conclusions reached in this book are entirely the author's.

CONTENTS: Pg

CHAPTER 1. OPENING SHOTS 13

CHAPTER 2. ROSMEAD, N. CAPE 18

CHAPTER 3. PRETORIA, THE SHOOTDOWN 20

CHAPTER 4. OATHS OF SILENCE 23

CHAPTER 5. INTERVIEW U.S.A. 25

CHAPTER 6. SEQUENCE OF EVENTS 27

CHAPTER 7. 30 DEG LATITUDE, 30 DEG LONGITUDE 29

CHAPTER 8. HOW CAN SOUTH AFRICA AND THE WORLD BENEFIT 33

CHAPTER 9. ANSWERING SOME QUESTIONS 35

CHAPTER 10. AREA 51 38

CHAPTER 1. OPENING SHOTS

The morning was still dark and cold as the cattle made their way to the milking parlour. Abantwana, the chief herdsman cracked his whip to keep them in line and moving. He had been chief herdsman for 15 years on the farm Kleinhoek. This winter morning seemed no different than any other, the milk smell hung in the chill winter morning like a blanket over his shoulders. The other younger herd boys waited for his further instruction as they too cracked their whips to guide the cattle into the "crush" which took them on to the parlour.

The "baas" of the farm Jaap Cronje was still sleeping and did not need to be awakened yet as he had full confidence in Abantwana. Apart from the occasional bellow of a cow, the milking progressed in silence. Jaap then joined the "milking party" and started asking the usual questions to which Abantwana had to answer "Ja baas or Nee baas."

TRANSLATION:

"Baas- Boss"

"Ja- Yes"

"Nee- No"

The milking completed Abantwana and the other herdsmen made their way to their huts for a welcome cup of tea, likewise Jaap made his way to the farmhouse to join his wife Ilsa for their morning tea. He and Ilsa had been married now for 18 years and were still happily married.

Daylight was starting to filter through the clouds as Abantwana approached the first "oats land"- a flat field planted with oats to feed the cattle through the lean, cold winter months. He looked over to his left and there, just sitting in the field was the strangest looking craft he had ever seen. The other herd boys had seen it too and had stopped dead in their tracks. They stood and stared at this strange craft for nearly 2 minutes before Abantwana instructed "Stompie"- the smallest herd boy to run to the farm and fetch the "Baas."

Jaap had just finished his tea when he happened to glance through the lounge window and saw "Stompie" running towards the farmhouse as fast as his little legs could carry him. "I wonder what could have got them so exited, thought Jaap- in all the years he had never seen them get worked up about anything, even when cattle had broken their legs."

Jaap met him at the door and tried to get him to calm down but all he heard was some strange looking aeroplane had crashed in his field of oats. "Damn, thought Jaap, I better go and see if there are any survivors but I must phone Colonel Sharp of the local police first to inform him of this trespasser on my land."

The time was just about 10 a.m. when Jaap and "Stompie" joined the others from their vigil on the hill. "Hell, thought

Jaap, that's no aeroplane but a bloody U.F.O." Jaap had never believed in U.F.O.'s but here was one right on his farm in broad daylight. The U.F.O. was round, metallic in colour with "port holes" all around the outside. It had three little pokey legs sticking out the bottom which were planted firmly on the ground.

Colonel Sharp now arrived in his police land rover and got out carrying his police issue .303 shotgun which he duly quickly loaded. The .303 slug is a massive bullet, capable of causing terrible damage to anything or anyone in it's path. Colonel Sharp's assistant, a heavy set Xhosa who carried a red flag was to be the "spotter."

Colonel Sharp quickly summed up the situation and remarked, "We must get rid of this unwelcome visitor." He then strode forward to within 75 meters of the U.F.O., aimed quickly and emptied the shotgun's rounds directly into the U.F.O. The bullets smashed into the U.F.O. with a metallic, clanging sound which echoed across the field. The U.F.O. quickly and silently shot into the air and “hovered” towards another field. Colonel Sharp shouted to his assistant, “Follow him and lift your flag so I know where you are.” The U.F.O. was duly followed to the next field where it now sat as before. Colonel Sharp had reloaded and again fired directly at the U.F.O. which now took off travelling westwards and disappeared.

The time was now 11 a.m.

CHAPTER 2. ROSMEAD, N. CAPE

Mrs. Roux, the Principal of Rosmead Primary School, having just finished a teachers meeting walked outside to enjoy some fresh air and sunshine. The Afrikaans and Math teachers joined her on her sojourn.

Simultaneously they all glanced towards the tennis courts and there hovering 20 meters or so above was the U.F.O. "Oh my God is that a U.F.O. exclaimed Mrs. Roux?" "It is indeed, muttered the other two teachers."

They all watched as the U.F.O. gently lowered itself to the surface with a hissing sound. Mrs. Roux was the first to react to the situation, "I'll go and alert the Police and Airforce, they need to take care of this "thing." The other two teachers simply stood and stared at this strange looking craft.

Five minutes later a Police van roared into sight- the occupants of the U.F.O.

seemed to have seen them as with flames now spouting from the bottom of the craft they into the air and disappeared.

The Police and teachers now walked over to the tennis courts to inspect the damage- there were three "welts" melted into the tarmac where the three legs had stood. There was a smell of Sulphur in the air and a strange stillness, almost as if time was standing still.

Newspapermen and radio personnel descended quickly on the small rural town of Rosmead with their cameras and microphones.

It was now nearly midday.

CHAPTER 3. PRETORIA, THE SHOOTDOWN.

Lieutenant Blignaut was busy with his routine radar sweep above Pretoria at 14h00 when he got the frantic call from his Commanding Officer George Snyman. "Top priority, be on the lookout for an unidentified craft approaching from the South- you are to guide the Mirage Jet Fighters to contact point for a shoot down." These were the strict orders of the then Prime Minister B.J. Vorster.

After all the commotion of the day's proceedings, word had reached the highest level and action needed to be taken- to "take out" this U.F.O. which had entered South African airspace illegally.

"I spotted the U.F.O. after coming through cloud cover just north of Pretoria and immediately noticed that this craft was in trouble, it was kind of wobbling in the sky." "I was under implicit orders to take it out so I opened up with both 20mm canon guns which ripped into the side of the U.F.O." "The U.F.O. went into a steep dive and crashed below me." "I decided to go down and take a look at this strange craft."

"The occupants of the U.F.O. were all dead- the technology and computers aboard that craft are what we are only seeing today." "The craft and occupants were ordered by the government to be sent to the U.S.A."

EXTRACTS FROM INTERVIEW WITH MIRAGE JET FIGHTER PILOT, CAPTAIN JOHAN BOTHA, NOVEMBER, 2008 RADIO ALGOA.

In summing up South Africa "gave away" her most prized possession in history to the U.S.A. The world was sold on the popular idea that the computer revolution started in the U.S.A. in 1975 but that's not true- the computer revolution started in South Africa in a little town in the Eastern Cape- Fort Beaufort in 1971.

Shortly after this “incident” Prime Minister B.J. Vorster had a heart attack and died in the Provincial Hospital, Port Elizabeth.

CHAPTER 4 OATHS OF SILENCE

An oath of silence is deemed necessary by a government if the security and integrity of the country are threatened and it's in the best interests of its people not to know the truth. An oath of silence stays in place for 30 years- by this time the government hopes that people would have forgotten the incident and that many of the witnesses would have passed away. In exchange for their silence the government pays out these key witnesses vast sums of money, even by today's standards it was still a lot of money that was payed out. These key witnesses (those still alive today) live in magnificent opulence at various estates around the country and overseas.

So, key witnesses (those still alive) were aloud by law to speak out about their experiences by 2001. The farmer (Jaap Cronje) and the Captain of the Mirage Jet (Johan Botha) were interviewed on radio Algoa in November, 2008. Strangely enough this interview was cut short so not too much information is known by the general public. According to friends Jaap Cronje swore on his death bed he was telling the truth when pressed by his friends in Port Alfred in December, 2009.

International Governments no longer try to cover up information regarding U.F.O.'s and lots of incidents throughout history can be found on the internet.

To contradict the above, the American people demanded that the Government conduct an official inquiry into the world famous Roswell, New Mexico U.F.O. crash of 1947. (America conducted the world's first nuclear bomb test in New Mexico in 1945.) The then American president in 2005, George Bush agreed and such an inquiry was conducted. Again, strangely enough the Government used the same lie as it did in 1945 claiming it was a weather balloon. The American Government used the same oaths of silence to keep key witnesses quite.

CHAPTER 5. INTERVIEW U.S.A.

Delegates from the American Press Corps descended on the small town of Fort Beaufort where all of the witnesses to the U.F.O. incident were interviewed. The substance of these interviews is known only by the American government.

Some of the questions which must have been asked are:

Why did the U.F.O. choose to land on your farm in particular?

What was your first reaction upon seeing the U.F.O.?

Did you think they were friendly?

If the Aliens were indeed friendly why did they not land at Port Elizabeth airport and introduce themselves?

Why did you shoot at the U.F.O.?

Why do you think the U.F.O. took off and landed again on another field?

Why did you shoot again at the U.F.O.?

What did you think when the U.F.O. took off and now disappeared from sight?

What was your first reaction upon seeing the U.F.O. land on the tennis court?

What was your first reaction upon seeing the U.F.O. lift off the tennis court and disappear from sight?

What was your first reaction upon seeing the U.F.O. after coming through cloud cover?

Why did you use bullets instead of heat seeking missiles to down the U.F.O.?

What did you think when you saw the dead aliens and a craft thousands of years more advanced than our own with all of that sophisticated computer technology on board?

Are aliens similar to us?

CHAPTER 6. SEQUENCE OF EVENTS

The sequence of events from a human perspective is exactly as described in previous chapters and was handled according to what each circumstance presented.

The sequence of events from an alien perspective must have been entirely different and could have gone like this:

Coming out of the "wormhole" on the "free electric intergalactic highway" and encountering some of the most beautiful land in the universe they now were looking for a "flat" area to land their craft. They saw the perfect spot- the farmer's oat field which was absolutely ideal as it also was a distance from interfering civilization. Unfortunately they were spotted but did not perceive imminent danger even when the Colonel approached with his "pointed stick." The damage caused by the bullets was a complete surprise and enormous shock to the aliens. Their craft was now fatally wounded and they needed to get away quickly to repair the damage which they tried unsuccessfully to do in another field but again were attacked so this time they hovered to another location, somewhere remote where they could repair their craft in peace. Again they were looking for a "flat" area to land and spotted the tennis court which looked perfect. This time they did not perceive the damage caused by the melted tar as it was sucked into their turbines when again they had to evacuate as humans had spotted them again. Their craft was now irreparable which meant it was impossible to get back onto the "intergalactic highway" and flee planet earth. As their craft was now a "sitting duck" even to earthly jet fighters their only option was to "hand themselves over" to the rulers of this land- South Africa. The craft and its alien occupants now tried to "hobble" to Pretoria but were blown out of the sky with no survivors.

CHAPTER 7. 30 DEGREES LATITUDE, 30 DEGREES LONGITUDE.

These coordinates are critical to understanding U.F.O. activity around the world. To completely understand this we need to look at the basic generation of electricity. To generate electricity you need a solenoid which is a metal armature with many copper coils- this armature needs to rotate at speed and sweep past the North and South pole of a magnet so giving rise to AC current. Each time the armature sweeps past the poles you get a "peak" or a "trough" which is alternating current.

The earth itself does this as it rotates on it's axis at 530Km/h every 24 hours with the "core or solenoid" sweeping past the North and South pole creating enormous "free electricity" which is concentrated at 30 degrees latitude, 30 degrees longitude. If you stood with a compass at the apex of (30,30), the compass needle will spin rapidly out of control due to the massive electrical and magnetic fluxes. This could be experienced at the exact spot where the U.F.O. landed on Jaap Cronje's farm outside Fort Beaufort. All over the world, areas with these coordinates have experienced massive, unbelievable U.F.O. activity.

Probably the most well known case in history is the disappearance of flight 19 over the Bahamas in December 1945 while on a routine training mission. (The Bermuda Triangle is located at approximately 30 degrees latitude, 30 degrees longitude and includes the Bahamas.) According to the report Captain Mark Taylor led his squadron out on a beautiful, sunny afternoon flying from Miami to Florida when at exactly 15h30 black clouds rolled in from all sides, his compass started spinning wildly and they lost all sense of direction. His last known report was: "Don't come after me, they look like they are from outer space." The subsequent rescue mission (a whole squadron of planes also flew into oblivion.) No sign of plane wreckage was ever found. A near miss happened again over the Bermuda Triangle in the 1970's when a Boeing passenger jet was also confronted with the black clouds at exactly 15h30 and his compass spinning wildly but this time the Captain managed to spot a tunnel of light and flew out of the catastrophe.

The time frame for this massive electrical-magnetic flux in the Northern hemisphere is 15h30, the mirror image clockwise in the Southern hemisphere is 9h30- about the time the U.F.O. landed on Jaap Cronje's farm near Fort Beaufort.

Some other places to experience massive U.F.O. activity are:

Arecibo- Puerto Rica

Darling-Australia

Salisbury-Zimbabwe

Hunan Province-China

Lausanne-Switzerland

Embrun-France

Rio de Oro-Northwest Africa

Grenada-Spain

Portalegre-Portugal

Teheran-Iran

Gotland-Sweden

South Island-New Zealand

New Hampshire-U.K.

Gdansk-Poland

Caracas-Venezuela.

CHAPTER 8. HOW CAN S.A. AND THE WORLD BENEFIT

South Africa will need to find a means of capturing this “free electricity” at (30, 30), almost like a “dream capture net.”This would have to be installed by satellite, making S.A. the first country in the world to use this technology. This will produce enough electricity for the entire country’s needs and cut the cost of electricity in half, making S.A. the country with the cheapest electricity. This “power station” near Fort Beaufort would provide jobs for millions of people and convert Fort Beaufort into a city overnight which will be known as the Fort Beaufort- Grahamstown metropole. This could happen as early as 2030.

This technology (to capture free electricity at 30, 30), could then be sold to the rest of the world and in so doing solve the world’s energy crisis once and for all. All this thanks to a U.F.O. which landed at Fort Beaufort 40 years ago which the government wanted everyone to forget about, not to mention the computer technology which should have belonged to S.A. and not to the U.S.A.

CHAPTER 9. ANSWERING SOME QUESTIONS

The reason why International governments threaten to "take away" a radio station's broadcasting license for reporting U.F.O. activity all has to do with he word "govern."To govern is to rule/reign/control. The key word is "control.' They need to control the airwaves; they need to control what people are allowed to hear. They do not want people to panic and create havoc.

The first time in history this happened was when Neil Armstrong landed on the moon in 1969. People who had "tuned" in on "ham radios" were able to hear his "uncensored" reporting of U.F.O.'s on the moon. These people were able to bypass the government control of the airwaves. International governments hate U.F.O.'s because they cannot control them. They enter a country's airspace illegally and use "free electricity." They "steal" livestock from farmers (cattle mutilations all around the world). They are normally too advanced for our jet fighters and can avoid capture by "disappearing" into another dimension.

The reason why the U.F.O. landed on a farm (Kleinhoek) near Fort Beaufort is because the farm is situated at the apex of 30 degrees latitude and 30 degrees longitude- the entrance and exit of the intergalactic highway.

Because the U.F.O. was a "sitting duck" for the Mirage Jet a heat seeking missile or bullets would have been equally effective in destroying it, it is a known fact in modern aerial combat that bullets are more effective in destroying enemy craft as they can still evade the heat seeking missile but they cannot evade bullets. From Vietnam to Iraq this has been proven over and over again.

U.F.O.'s have visited earth at various locations around the globe at 30 degrees latitude, 30 degrees longitude but for reasons other than nuclear disarmament.

Some of these reasons are:

To check on our technological progress.

To use male and female humans in breeding experiments (cross breeding). [Abductions reported all over the world.]

To allow as many people on earth as possible to see them and witness their craft and to set their minds free from their prison on earth. [Billions of people around the globe have now witnessed U.F.O.'s]

To communicate their existence to us- crop circles all over the world.

Aliens are very much like us- we are all a product of the same universe. A theory goes that aliens made us from D.N.A., in other words we are their children. This theory is supported by the fact that we are in actual fact aliens on planet earth- if you took away all the man-made structures and artifacts the earth would return to it's natural state. We don't really belong here- we are aliens on earth.

CHAPTER 10. AREA 51

Area 51, Nevada Desert, U.S.A. - the most heavily fortified, secure place on earth. Area 51 is "sold" to the general public as a top secret military test facility administered as Detachment 3 of the Edwards Air Force Base, California. Other names given to the area include: The Skunkworks, Dreamland, Groom Lake Military Base, Watertown, The Ranch, Paradise Ranch and The Box. The main UFOlogy interest in the base at Groom Lake comes from the belief that the debris and bodies from the Roswell Incident were taken to the area 51 for reverse engineering and autopsies respectively.

The Fort Beaufort U.F.O. and occupants were in all likelihood taken to area 51 also for reverse engineering and autopsies. Extraterrestrial Highway 375 and the town of Rachel, the "U.F.O. Capital of the World" are nearby. There is a restricted area within 14 miles of the facility marked by signs which notify you that the security are authorized to use deadly force. Only persons with Presidential clearance are allowed in.

So what is area 51 and what happens there? Area 51 is the area set aside by the U.S. military and government for alien contact. Here the best scientists in the world are working side by side with alien scientists on the most pressing problems facing planet earth. These scientists together with their families live and work here- they have all the facilities and comforts of a normal family. They are hardly ever allowed to leave. Problems such as aids, cancer, global warming, food supply, energy, recycling, e.t.c. are being tackled.

Often in the night sky over the Nevada Desert U.F.O.'s can be seen landing and taking off.